Catch The Guy

Real World Dating Advice for Women on How to Be Irresistible & Attract The Man You Want

Glenna D. Waldo
Copyright© 2015 by Glenna D. Waldo

Catch The Guy

Publisher: Enlightened Publishing

ISBN-13: 978-1508699385

ISBN-10: 1508699380

Disclaimer

The Publisher has strived to be as accurate and complete as possible in the creation of this book. While all attempts have been made to verify information provided in this publication, the Publisher assumes no responsibility for errors, omissions, or contrary interpretation of the subject matter herein. Any perceived slights of specific persons, peoples, or organizations are unintentional.

This book is not intended for use as a source of legal, business, accounting or financial advice. All readers are advised to seek services of competent professionals in the legal, business, accounting, and finance fields.

The information in this book is not intended or implied to be a substitute for professional medical advice, diagnosis or treatment. All content contained in this book is for general information purposes only. Always consult your healthcare provider before carrying on any health program.

Table of Contents

Introduction

Are you ready to start letting love enter your life?

For those who haven't been so lucky in love, starting anew can be harder than anything else they have tried. Especially if someone has just gotten out of a long term relationship, getting back into the dating scene can be a daunting task. Before you are ready to start looking for love, you need to make sure that you are ready for it again, or maybe even for the first time. Being open to love means you have to be mentally and emotionally ready for anything, even if that means getting your heart broken. If you are not ready to completely put yourself out there, finding the right person will be much more difficult.

You cannot hold a grudge towards the opposite sex, nor can you still be grieving over the loss of an ex. This frame of mind will not lead to successful dates, no matter how great the guy is, and will essentially set you up to fail. It is even possible that potential dates will sense this hostility and back-out of plans they have already made with you, or decide not to approach you in the first place.

That being said, this book (though wonderful) is not a miracle worker. If you are not in a healthy, open and accepting state of mind, even the best suggestions out there become useless. Let go of past heartbreak, disappointments, and apprehensions. Gather your confidence, prioritize what is most important to you, and figure out what you are really looking for out of life. This book can hold all the advice that you need in order to find Mr.Right, but if you are not receptive to the idea, Mr.Right will always be Mr.Wrong.

Are you really ready? Are you sure? Then it's time to start fresh with the new rules of dating!

Chapter 1 – The New Rules of Dating

Things are no longer the same as they were in the 1950's. Men no longer expect all women to be demure, innocent, house wives-in-training. In fact, behaving in that way can sometimes harm your chances of getting a second date. If you do happen to be naturally shy, quiet, and love to cook and clean, there are surely men out there who will love you for it. However, if you are an ambitious, out-spoken career woman, be yourself! It shouldn't be hard to find a man that will be enamored with your go-getter attitude. It's all about attracting the right kind of mate to suit you.

Here are the new rules you need to know.

- **You don't have to wait to ask him out**. Many men would actually feel relieved if you did the asking. Though once seen as a sign of desperation, a lady who asks the guy out appears confident, outgoing, and brave. With qualities like that, it would be pretty hard for any guy to turn you down. The worst that could happen is he is otherwise committed or simply says "No thanks." Learning to overcome rejection is just a part of life, and though it may not feel great at the time, it will inevitably make you a stronger person. So what's the big deal? Like him? Ask him out!

- **"Taking it slow" is relative.** Don't be afraid to jump right in - not into the sack necessarily, but don't think there is some general rule to follow when it comes to the physical aspect of a relationship. Men who are only looking for sex will simply leave, and guys that really like you will stick around no matter how fast things go. Just be honest with yourself. If you sleep with someone on the first or second date and you don't hear from them again, be prepared to accept it. This may be just fine for ladies who are not looking to get super serious right off the bat. For those who are really trying to avoid that situation, make sure you take enough time to get to know a guy and his intentions before having sex.

- **You'll need to ask your date what they are looking for in a relationship with you**. Casual sex and open relationships are now a lot more common than they ever were before. During our parents' generation, a date was a date. That was it. It was a sign of relationship-status. Unfortunately, it's not that way anymore. It's best to know upfront what a guy wants out of a relationship before you commit yourself to a single person. It's a hurtful situation to be in when you find out you have been totally faithful to someone and they haven't been to you, even if it is a simple misunderstanding. This can also put you at risk for STDs. Though many men dread having "the relationship talk," it is in your best interest to find out beforehand if this guy is not even looking for a girlfriend, let alone a wife.

- **You need to be proactive about sexual safety**. 20 years ago, sexual safety wasn't such a big issue. Nowadays, a lot more people are STD-positive, and if you want to stay disease-free, you need to make an effort to learn your partner's sexual history. Though it's often a difficult topic to present and an all-around awkward conversation, it is vital to your health nonetheless. If a guy is very up-front with you and happily answers your questions without hesitation, that's usually a good sign he also takes this matter seriously, and will do the same for you. However, you always have to protect yourself. Of course using a condom is a no-brainer, but no method of protection against STDs (or birth control, for that matter) is 100% effective. Choose your sexual partners with care, and if anything seems sketchy, wait it out until you can trust him or just move on.

- **The First 48 tell volumes about what a guy thinks about you**. Those who aren't quite in the 20 to 30 age group might not have heard of the term known as "The First 48." The saying goes that the first 48 hours after giving a guy your phone number will reveal if he is really interested in you. If he calls in 2 days, he wants you. If not, you shouldn't waste too much time or energy waiting for that call. He was either too drunk when he got your number, chickened-out, or was just showing off to his friends. Get back out there until you find someone who just can't wait to talk to you.

- **Scope out his social media**. If you see signs that he's a neighborhood Lothario, just RUN! Too many women flirting with him, as well as too many not-so-cool comments from him could be a sign of a cheater waiting to happen. Just make sure you give him a shot. Maybe he is a photographer who works with beautiful models every day and their contact truly is platonic, or grew up with sisters and has lots of female friends. Whatever the case, just proceed with caution, especially in terms of a physical relationship, until you figure out exactly what his deal is.

- **Keep your standards**. Don't let the new ways of dating fool you, you can still get the relationship that you want without all that hassle. Don't let any kind of guy sway you into lowering the bar. It will only hurt you in the end. Trust your instincts and your heart to lead you in the right direction. It really is better to be single than to set yourself up for something you already know won't work out for the long haul. You only wind up wasting your time and ending up right where you began. On the flip side, you also have to realize when your standards are set impossibly high. It's unlikely that you will be able to find someone who fits an incredibly specific description. There are only so many 6 foot 4 inch tall, blonde, blue-eyed pediatric doctors who have never been married, don't have kids, love jazz, and have a six-pack. Staying open to possibilities is just as important as staying true to your standards. Unless that possibility is a 33 year old unemployed college drop-out who still lives at home with Mom.

- **If he doesn't have a job, he cannot afford you**. This is one rule that doesn't change over time. Meeting someone when they have just gotten laid off and being approached by a lazy, unemployment-collecting loser are two different scenarios. Learn to tell the difference. There is no need to automatically write-off a college graduate who is actively interviewing and looking for work every day. If this continues and he becomes complacent with the situation, or you are put under financial strain due to it, then it may be time to cut the cord. For guys who are perfectly happy taking you to the cheapest pizza place on the block and asking you to spend the night at their parents' house, don't even waste your time.

The Wrong "New Rules of Dating"

Though dating has changed a lot, some things definitely remain the same. Following every piece of advice from dating websites, TV shows, and anyone you talk to is not the smartest way to go. What works for someone else may not work for you, or they could be off-track all together. If you have been repeatedly turned down for dates, or find yourself gaining a negative reputation, it might be because you are not following the right rules of dating. Here are the rules that you need to avoid following, as well as the reasons why.

- *Guys love loose women, so it's okay to wear a short, skin-tight dress when you go out.* Giving the guy the wrong impression, or actually giving anyone the wrong impression, will only hurt your dating life. If you want to be taken seriously, do not show too much skin. Find the perfect balance of class and sex appeal, since leaving things to the imagination will only make him want more. If he doesn't, he is clearly only looking for sex. The general rule of thumb is to only show skin in one major area. If you are opting for a mini-skirt, keep a high neckline and sleeves. For low-cut tops or dresses, cover your legs and/or arms completely. Creating a focal point that draws attention to your best feature without giving everything away is alluring and shows you still have self-respect.

- *If I don't sleep with him, I will lose him!* Though it's alright to have sex if you want to, you should never, EVER, feel pressured into sex in order to keep a guy. If he is using you, he is not worth your time, and this could actually be a sign of something worse to come, like infidelity or potential abuse. If he is actually into you, he will stick around regardless of what happens between you physically, or how long it takes. A real gentleman will simply bring up the conversation before trying to get you into bed.

- *I should pay for everything on a date.* Going Dutch (halfsies) is certainly reasonable on a first date, and a lot of women won't even stand for that. If you are the one to ask a guy out, however, you should be prepared to pay just in case. This may not be ideal, and could potentially turn you off to him all together, but you expect a guy to pay if he asks you out, right? When it's the guy that approaches you and asks you on a date, it is chivalrous for him to cover the entire tab. If going Dutch makes you feel empowered, then go for it! If you like to be wooed, then your date at least offering to pay is a preliminary sign that you might be compatible.

- *Nightclubs are great places to meet men.* Usually, nightclubs are the place where singles go for a quick hookup. Not many people there are interested in more than a one night stand. Try to see clubs as a great place to let loose with friends, and possibly scope out a guy to go out with later. If you are truly looking for a relationship, and a guy approaches you at a club, don't just go home with him. Give him your number and tell him a restaurant you love or movie you have been waiting to see. If he is only looking for a hook-up, he won't bother. But if you get a call the next day to go see that movie, at least you have a chance to start with a real date and see where it goes.

- *Men are going to be OK with baggage.* Everyone has it. It's true. There is no baggage-free person. However, men aren't going to be OK with hearing it on the first couple of dates. Droning on and on about negative issues or past relationships is an instant turn-off to just about anyone. You wouldn't enjoy an evening of hearing about how his ex-girlfriend trashed him online and wouldn't give his dog back, so don't put him in that position. There is a big difference between getting to know someone and finding out about their sexual/relationship history and offering up unflattering information. Keeping conversation light and focusing on positive aspects like food, hobbies, career goals, and the like will let you know if you like someone enough to divulge such personal anecdotes, anyway.

- *Sexting is a good way to get a new guy interested*. Sexting, or sending nudes, is a great way to get a creep to blackmail you. If you don't believe it, ask Anthony Weiner about his escapades. When it comes to nude photos, don't send them unless you are ready for the world to see them. Never forget that information sent over the Internet can become available to just about anyone, at any time, without your knowledge or consent. If sending saucy photos is your thing, at least wait until you are in a monogamous, committed relationship; and even then, watch your back.

- *All of the guys on Internet dating sites are single.* Actually, it's a good idea to ask before you meet up with them. A good 33% of them are actually taken, and just looking for a fling. They certainly won't show up sporting a wedding ring or flashing photos of their kids. The last thing you want is someone's wife out to get you for dating her husband. Even with the best intentions and no knowledge of the situation, you are still partly at fault and could contribute to ending a marriage, or breaking up a family where kids are involved. Do your due diligence, too, because let's face it, if this guy is already lying about his relationship status, why is he going to come clean at the first inquiry? It is always in your best interest to be on high-alert when you date someone you met over the Internet.

Chapter 2 – Why Are You Single?

Behavioral signals are a big reason why many beautiful, successful women continue to remain single. You may not even realize that things you say, your actions, and even body language could be putting you at a disadvantage. Subconscious or learned behaviors as well as bad habits can result in creating a major road block in finding Mr. Right. Carefully examining yourself and past relationships can help you grow as a person and be that much more open to love. Acknowledging past mistakes or unhealthy thoughts and actions can shed light on past and present dating issues. If you have been wondering why men have not been checking you out, or why you never seem to get past that first or second date, consider these common mistakes that send the wrong signals.

Too Much Baggage

Men don't want to deal with drama before they even met you. If you have a history of suicide attempts, bad breakups, or even financial issues, keep it to yourself. Don't let people know how much you might have been hurt before they have an opportunity to hear your accomplishments. If everything they know about you is negative or makes you appear unstable, it doesn't exactly scream fun.

If a sensitive subject happens to come up in the beginning, try to quickly find a tangent towards something more positive, or simply be as honest as you can without victimizing yourself. For instance, if you had a rough home life growing up and your date asks about your family, offer something like "I don't have a relationship with my Dad, but I am super close with my Mom" and share a funny or interesting story about her to steer the conversation in a better direction.

Desperation

Though this is technically a form of baggage, desperation can turn even the most beautiful woman into an undesirable wreck.

No one wants to be a person's last pick, and no one wants to feel like they are the bottom of the barrel that you are settling with. It's human nature to want to choose someone who has standards, since it makes you appear superior to other mates. Desperation gets rid of standards, and is an unattractive quality in anyone. Even if you have been single (and celibate) for way too long, there is never any reason to feel desperate or lower your dating standards. If you decide to date someone that does not have the qualities you are looking for, you are setting yourself up to waste not only your own time, but his, as well.

Little Miss Ice Queen

Being an ice queen is a good way to get men to think that you would never be interested, even if you are. Have people told you that you have a very standoffish stance? Or, have they told you that you just seem uninterested in men? This dysfunction is mostly non-verbal communication, but it might also be the things you say that shut men out before they can talk to you. You might need to brush up on making yourself appear like a more open, accepting, and possibly even available woman.

Employ a good friend or two to come out to the bar and take note of your body language and facial expressions. Standing with your arms crossed and a furrowed brow all night definitely sends the wrong signals and can be intimidating to nice guys who would otherwise approach you. This may be subconscious behavior, which is why having someone you trust act as your social "mirror" can be helpful.

The Miss Match

The worst mistake that a woman can do is to look for love in all the wrong places. Opposites can attract just as long as you have something in common, too. If you are a preppy girl looking for a punk rock boyfriend, it's probably not going to happen. Are you an extrovert who likes introverted men? You may need to refine your searches to find someone who is more similar to you, your tastes, and your lifestyle choices before you start dating around some more.

Common interests are possibly one of the most important factors that lead to ultimate compatibility. If you continue to seek out mates you have nothing in common with, creating meaningful conversation, finding activities to do together, and building a foundation for a lasting relationship will get very difficult, very quickly.

The Fashion Disaster

Believe it or not, men are very receptive to what a woman wears. If you wear sloppy clothing, overly sleazy clothing, or simply clothing that doesn't flatter you the way it should, you're shooting yourself in the foot. Men want a woman who is fashionable, but not slutty. They want a woman who is put together, and also looks like she cares about her appearance. After all, most men stray when they feel their once-fashionable wife "let go of herself."

Looks aren't everything, and you certainly want to find someone who loves you for you, but presenting yourself in the best possible way will not only attract an equally put-together gentleman, but give you confidence, to boot. Keep hair clean and maintained, find clothes that fit properly, and most of all, keep to the utmost standards of personal hygiene. There is no need to look like a fashionista if that isn't who you are, but if you put on a little black dress that fits perfectly, you can't lose.

The Hyper Feminist

It's no secret that men can be intimidated by a feminist. Feminism can be a great thing, and women should always be treated as equals. However, most men will shrink away from a woman who appears hostile to the concept of even letting a guy pay for a date or open a door. Chivalry is often a sign that the guy you are with is a good pick. There is no need to oppose being treated with the highest level of care and respect. If you feel he is treating you like a fragile porcelain doll, show a little strength without making him feel threatened or put-down. Carry something heavy, open a jar with some elbow grease, or even open the door for him!

Ladies, pick your battles wisely. Let men be men, as long as it isn't hurting anyone. If you do end up with this guy down the road, traditional gentlemanly behavior is something you will really appreciate later in life.

Special Notes

Being single isn't necessarily a bad thing, but it can be for women who are not very happy with that status. A big complaint among women is that men seem to only want them for sex, or don't ever call after the first date.

Men who are not taking you out on 2nd dates might not be doing so because of the signals that you send. When looking for a girl-friend, guys tend to gravitate towards ladies who are down-to-earth, self-possessed, and have their own friends and interests (aka not clingy). Women who are wild, excitable, or just wacky usually will get cast aside. In other words, that kind of behavior may lead them to believe you are unstable.

If you are labeled as unstable, then there isn't much you can do to salvage the relation-ship. You can try to act as sane and as normal as possible, but the fact is that it won't do much to sway a man's mind on the subject. Instead, simply cut your losses, and try to figure out what you are doing wrong so that you won't do it again in the future.

Not sure what you are doing wrong? Some of these things mark instability in women to men:

- "Spilling your guts" about all your problems on the first date
- Bemoaning your last bunch of relationships to a point of redundancy
- Twitching and fidgeting constantly
- Saying flatly that you are a drug user
- Boasting about escapades you have done with your friends that might be considered to be immature, unstable, or ridiculous
- Acting accusatory or too defensive on a first date
- Crying or exhibiting unnecessary emotion
- Showing a sudden disinterest in the date, the activity, or anything else without a visible reason

While you should always be yourself, the best version of you doesn't have to include any of the less-than-attractive actions listed above. Sure, you will want to share your hopes, dreams, fears, and deepest secrets once you are in a relationship, but first dates are for making a good impression. Don't send the wrong message before you have the chance to send the right one.

Dating Profiles of Real Women

Having an outsider's perspective on someone's dating life can often be a window into your own. Below we'll take a look at dating profiles for 4 different women between the ages of 19 and 38. These real women all come from different backgrounds with their own ideas of how dating should be. See if you can tell what they may be doing wrong or right, and if any of these ladies sound a bit like you!

Shanna, 19 is a Professional Dancer and Choreographer in New York City, NY.

- **History**: Shanna has a busy, city lifestyle and unruly schedule due to booking new jobs and rehearsals. She is a bit shy, and does not have much dating experience. Though she casually dated a couple of guys in high school, she did not experience her first serious relationship until moving to the city a year ago. Shanna was with her boyfriend, Ricky, for 9 months and they lived together for 6. They broke-up due to him being older, at 24, and wanting to pursue things in life Shanna was not ready for. Newly single, Shanna is frequently approached by men due to her pretty face and lithe, dancer's figure.

- **Dating Scene**: Since Shanna is only 19, she is not necessarily looking for a serious relationship, but is open to one if the right guy comes along. She frequents her favorite midtown Manhattan restaurants and more upscale bars, and even goes out to a club every now and then. Working in a female-dominated industry with a constantly changing schedule leaves little time for her to find new places to meet guys. When going out with girlfriends, she typically wears her hair up, a nice pair of jeans, light blouse, and tailored jacket. Though she is shy, she tries to make the effort to talk to men who approach her, but is not afraid to say no if she feels she does not want to give out her number.

- **The Pros**: At a mere 19 years of age, Shanna has plenty of time to look for Mr. Right. She has also developed good habits in presenting herself in a positive and put-together way. With her first serious relationship under her belt, she is starting to figure out what she does and does not want in a partner.

- **The Cons**: Lack of life experience and a natural hesitation to put herself out there could potentially keep Shanna single for longer than she'd like. Although she has an unpredictable schedule, taking the initiative to go out to a bar or perusing the local bookstore when she has the chance should greatly increase her chances of meeting someone worthwhile.

- **The Verdict**: For the most part, Shanna is doing just about everything a 19 year old should be doing in the big-city dating scene. As long as she doesn't get caught-up in a bad relationship or compromise her inherent work ethic, she's bound to find Mr. Right!

Kathryn, 23 is an MBA graduate student at the University of Southern Georgia, GA.

- **History**: Kathryn is a hard-working, dedicated student with ambitious goals in the business world. She works part-time as an intern at a financial firm near her school, and is a member of the Delta Delta Delta Sorority. Between earning her master's degree, her internship, and obligations as a sorority sister, Kathryn doesn't have much time to date. She has always been outgoing and open to love, hoping to get married and start a family before turning 30. With a substantial amount of casual dating experience, Kathryn can easily tell after one date if she should see someone again, or not. She has also been in two serious relationships, one for two years of high school and one for 16 months in college. Kathryn ended both relationships due to her busy schedule and her boyfriend's lack of flexibility to work around it.

- **Dating Scene**: Since she is part of a sorority, most of Kathryn's activities revolve around other students on campus and partnering with fraternities. Her packed schedule leaves minimal time available to go seek out dates on her own terms. However, she always makes sure to style herself head to toe since she never really knows who she may run into. Kathryn's style is feminine and flirty, but very professional at her internship. She loves to wear pink, always styles her hair, and makes sure she has on plenty of make-up. Though frequently approached by men, she turns many of them down simply due to lack of free time and not wanting to waste the little time she has available.

- **The Pros**: Kathryn is put-together, smart, ambitious, and outgoing. These are all great qualities for the dating world, and make her seem like a catch to the type of guy she is hoping to attract. Working in a professional office gives Kathryn an idea of the guy she hopes to find, and she does not waste her time with anyone that does not live up to her high standards.

- **The Cons**: Though Kathryn's unabashed, motivated personality can be great, it can also be very intimidating to potential suitors. Her somewhat demanding nature that ended her two previous relationships can be another hurdle in her deadline to be married and a mom by the age of 30. She also needs to be aware of how she presents herself at sorority functions. A heavy layer of make-up and micro-mini skirt may be OK for her 18 year old sorority sisters, but will only attract sleazy frat guys and just isn't the right look for her.

- **The Verdict**: As far as her love life goes, it would be in Kathryn's best interest to be a bit more open and less controlling when it comes to potential partners. Having almost unattainably high dating standards combined with a lack of free time to make herself available outside of work and school has left her in a bit of a rut. Finding the love of her life, marrying him, and having a baby within the next 6 years is a tall order. Staying open-minded to guys outside of the business world and taking herself a little less seriously will increase her chances of finding Mr. Right. Once she does, it's up to her to compromise a bit more, and make time for the relationship, instead of expecting everything to revolve around her.

Rachel, 28 is a fashion designer and clothing line owner in Los Angeles, CA.

- **History**: Rachel is a creative and free-spirited Southern California fashion designer. Owning her own business means making her own schedule and having lots of time for friends and dating. She started dating at the early age of 13, and hasn't slowed down since. With ample experience in both casual and serious dating, and nearly 5 years in her longest relationship, Rachel has a pretty clear picture of what she's looking for. Though Rachel has experienced some serious heartbreak after the end of her 5 year long relationship, followed by an intense on again, off again romance for nearly a year, she takes little baggage into her current dating life. Though she would like to get married and have kids someday, she feels there is no rush while still in her twenties.

- **Dating Scene:** Living in the spread-out metropolitan city of Los Angeles means there are lots of options for twenty-something's looking to meet people. Since Rachel already frequents all of the age-appropriate hot spots, finding Mr. Right is really a matter of discretion. As a fashion designer, she always looks modern, sleek, and perfectly put-together when going out to a restaurant or bar. She also frequently goes to concerts, the beach, and walking around her West LA neighborhood. She has been single for almost 2 years, but for the last six months has been casually dating two guys at the same time. Neither knew about the other, nor have they tried to discuss where the relationship is going, or if it is even exclusive.

- **The Pros:** Being a business owner with a flexible schedule is a great asset in the dating world, as well as looking the part. With impeccable fashion sense, Rachel is sending the right message to the guys she hopes to attract. Her carefree spirit is also a positive factor, especially when meeting someone for the first time.

- **The Cons**: Dating two guys at the same time is risky business. At this point she should be able to tell which one she can see a future with, and simply end things with the other before he asks her to commit. Continuing to prolong dating two people casually instead of getting serious with one could leave her single and childless well into her thirties, and end up losing two great guys.

- **The Verdict**: When it comes to Rachel's love life, she seems to be avoiding commitment. This could be due to hesitation from past heartbreak, or wanting to wait longer to make sure she chooses the right guy to get serious with. At some point, however, she will have to choose or risk losing both guys, who could have potentially been that life partner she hopes to have one day. With nearly everything else going for her, it would be in Rachel's best interest to have a conversation with each guy and see where they are coming from. This could shed some light on which one she has stronger feelings for, and which one may work out in the long run, if either. If not, it's time to cut the cord and move on. There are plenty of single guys in Los Angeles, after all.

Bridget, 38 is a Registered Nurse Practitioner in St. Louis, MO.

- **History**: Bridget is a warm, loving nurse practitioner who is very devoted to her career and religion. When she is not at work, she is probably at church, volunteering, or spending time with her family, all of whom live nearby. An old-fashioned girl, Bridget has not done too much casual dating, and only had two long-term relationships, one for 2 years, and one for 5 years, with the latter culminating in an engagement. When her fiancé broke-off their engagement six months before their wedding, Bridget was devastated. Now, three years later, she hopes to still find her Mr. Right, settle down, and start a family. Since family and religious values are so important to her, Bridget has not had an easy time finding a like-minded man.

- **Dating Scene**: With a steady job, good income, and set schedule, it should be easy enough for Bridget to make time for dating. However, due to her values and interests, she often frequents inconvenient spots for meeting men. Spending a lot of time at her childhood home as well as with married siblings who have children doesn't really encourage her to frequent single hot spots. Bridget may be conservative, but makes an effort to stay fashionable and look put-together when going to church or spend time with family. Since she is not often in the right setting, she does not get approached my men very often, and when she does, is hesitant to give them her number.

- **The Pros**: Having values and a good job bodes well for Bridget, and puts her in a good position to look for a serious relationship. Her down-to-earth personality and warm, friendly energy make her even more attractive to the mid-thirties men she is hoping to find.

- **The Cons**: A broken engagement naturally comes with a lot of baggage.

Though it has already been 3 years, it is difficult not to be jaded by that kind of heartbreak. Her age is also a factor, and edging closer to that mid-thirties mark could seem undesirable even for a guy who may be a few years older. It also makes her more eager to move into a relationship and address where it is going too quickly.

- **The Verdict**: If Bridget really wants to find Mr. Right while she can have time to make sure he's The One and start a family, she may have to get out of her comfort zone. Meeting a guy at church would be great, but at this point she already knows just about everyone; and they are mostly married. Taking some time to grab dinner with a couple of girlfriends, go shop on her own in a nice department or book store, or even have a drink alone at an upscale bar would increase her chances of meeting someone. She should also consider joining a specific dating site like Christian Mingle, to pinpoint the type of guy she's looking for.

Chapter 3 – The Meeting Places

Meeting single men is a lot easier than you would think, but you should look for men in the right places. What you are looking for in a guy will tell you where you should start looking, and it will also tell you what areas you should avoid in order to keep away from Mr. Wrong.

Though bars and clubs are standard meeting places, they are most commonly seen by men as the spot to find "hook-ups" or "one night stands." Keep your eyes open when frequenting your favorite places of interest. You never know who may walk through the door of your local bookstore, gym, specialty grocery store, or church. This way, at least you know right off the bat you and your potential date have something in common. The type of guy you are interested in will steer you in the right direction, and reveal which places you may want to avoid.

The Gym Fiend

Are physical fitness and overall health top priorities in your life? Then the gym may be the perfect place to go to find your Mr. Right (or Mr. Right Now). Guys don't mind sweat, so don't be afraid to commit to a treadmill run, lifting heavy weights, and showing your strength. Your dedication should attract a guy with a similar mindset, and maybe impress him a bit, too! So pick up a barbell and start pumping iron. You will be bound to find a guy interested in talking to you if you work out in a nice gym.

- *YOU CAN ALSO TRY*: Bike races, marathons, spas, yoga classes, public pools, and local adult sports leagues, such as softball..

- *AVOID*: Anything that involves a lot of sedentary or unhealthy activities, such as gaming conventions, lectures, crafting classes, and fast food joints.

Mr. Rich and Successful

You will need to look for education if you are looking for a man who is financially successful. Going to college is one of the easiest places to find a future Bill Gates, and it's a great way to learn volumes about what successful men are really looking for in a woman. Besides which, educated guys are just about always looking for an educated mate. Even if you fantasize about marrying rich and being a fantastic mother and housewife, having your own avenues to support yourself and professional ambitions are attractive qualities to a successful career man. If you are a current college student, keep yourself looking professional and put together for every class - today just might be the day that cute guy notices you. If you are not in school, consider signing up for some community college or local recreation classes that interest you or could help advance your current profession.

- *YOU CAN ALSO TRY*: Investing clubs, finance workshops, on the job, and classes that deal with business owner skills. Special dating sites also cater to this kind of man, but be on alert for Mr. Right Now's.

- *AVOID*: Don't go anywhere that doesn't attract affluent people. Avoid cheap bars, inner city hangouts, and low-end shopping malls.

Mr. Family Man

If you are looking for a guy who wants to settle down with a woman, you are looking for a guy who has moral scruples. You're not going to find anywhere that has better selection than through a local church community. Churchgoing men have been statistically linked to higher marriage rates. It doesn't matter what your religion might be, either. If you do have religious stipulations for your mate, and are not having any luck in your current community, try participating in a weekly service at another local church or temple, and scope out guys without a wedding ring or obvious significant other.

- *YOU CAN ALSO TRY*: Colleges, community service clubs, volunteer organizations, and religion-specific dating sites.

- *AVOID*: Nightclubs, bars, frat parties, and just about anything even remotely sleazy. Even if you did meet a family-oriented man at one of these locations, he may not take you seriously purely based on where you met.

Mr. Stud

You can find a hot man who is interested in you for a one night stand almost anywhere. If you are open to it, just make sure you look put-together, with the perfect blend of sex appeal and class. Even if you are looking for a hook-up, there is never any reason to look trashy. Keep your body language warm and inviting, and smile as much as possible. It won't take long for a hottie in the bar to notice that beautiful smile and approach you.

- *YOU CAN ALSO TRY*: Online dating sites like Tinder or Zoosk, mixers, speed dating, nightclubs, and bars. Almost anywhere is a good place to search, within reason. Just make sure to be safe if you decide to go home with a guy you meet on the Internet.

- *AVOID*: Anything that is too family-oriented. Churches, college lectures, and matchmaker sites are generally not a good place to find Mr. Right Now's.

Mr. Popular

Mr. Popular is both a ladies' man and a man's man - men want to be him, and women want to be with him. This is the guy who people naturally gravitate to during a party, and is often the guy who people are naturally envious of. He is well dressed, has a great sense of humor, always seems cheerful, and just has more friends than he can count! For a budding socialite, this is the perfect match. It should be noted that many Mr. Populars are serial cheaters, though, so watch out! You're bound to find this cutie pie in the center of any party, convention, or dance club. This category also covers rock stars, celebs, and similar folk.

- *YOU CAN ALSO TRY*: Trying to find Mr. Popular can actually also happen at debutante balls, social affairs like fashion shows, concerts, and even on photo shoots. Remember, this guy wants to be the center of attention 24/7.

- *AVOID*: Avoid introverted places, such as libraries. If you aren't looking for a Mr. Right Now, then you need to avoid clubs. Men in clubs are almost never looking for their future wife – and if they are, you have to wonder.

NOTE: If you choose to chase Mr. Popular, you will have a LOT on your hands. Jealous women will try to snag him from you, and you will have to have a lot of confidence in order to deal with the cattiness that can happen when you date a popular guy. It's quite sad, but it's a bad side effect of popularity.

Mr. Brainy

Mr. Brainy often is a man who is quiet, but well-spoken. If you are looking for an intellectual or a self-proclaimed nerd, you are going to be pleased. Geeky guys, as well as brainy boys, usually have higher salaries and higher marriage rates. Optometrists in particular have very low divorce rates. Faithful, thankful, and always sweet, smart men are often found in forums, libraries, and anywhere that can offer them the intellectual stimulation that they crave, including colleges, art schools, and specialized classes.

- *YOU CAN ALSO TRY*: Gaming and technology conventions, multicultural events, live theaters, educational lectures, and similar social arenas.

- *AVOID*: Avoid clubs, bars, and anywhere that seems kind of...well, stupid. Use your common sense in this matter. If you can't get something out of it intellectually, he won't, either.

Chapter 4 – Online Dating

Online dating sites become more popular each year, and are setting the new standard for busy professionals to meet eligible singles. While there are many dangers and pitfalls associated with online dating, there are just as many success stories and eventual marriages.

Before putting yourself out there on a dating site, make sure you choose the right site for you, take precautions to protect yourself, and reveal just enough information to attract the type of guy you really want. Whether you turn to online dating sites in lieu of time to go out and meet people, being too shy to approach someone in person, or just want to see what all of the fuss is about, make sure it's the right move for you.

Choosing the Right Site

So you have decided that online dating is a good fit for your love life. Now you have to take a careful look at several dating sites to make sure you choose the service that best suits your needs. New dating sites pop up frequently, but established sites are generally the way to go. It can be helpful to make a list of what you are looking to find, and what is most important to you. Then, as you visit some dating sites, see which ones fit most closely with your criteria.

For the most part, online dating sites can be broken down into several categories, with a couple of stand-outs in each one.

- **Singles looking for a fun fling that could turn into a relationship: Zoosk, Tinder, Plenty of Fish**. For younger singles who just want to get out in the dating scene, meet people for fun, and possibly end up with a boyfriend or girlfriend, these sites are a good start. Zoosk and Plenty of Fish tend to be more geared towards finding one person to stay with, while Tinder is sometimes seen as more of a "hook-up" site. If you are not too serious about finding

Mr. Right and getting a ring your finger ASAP, then one of these sites could be right for you.

- **Commitment minded singles focused on finding a life partner: eHarmony, Match.com**. These types of sites are often geared towards singles in their mid-twenties through early forties, and have some of the highest online marriage rates around. Their lengthy questionnaires may seem tedious, but claim to help find that deep connection needed to find Mr. (or Mrs.) Right. It is often assumed that singles on these sites have chosen them specifically to help find their future life partner. If that's what you are looking for, these sites are probably a good fit for you.

- **Religious singles set on marrying someone within their own faith: JDate, Christian Mingle**. Whether it is important to you or your family that you marry someone who shares your religious beliefs, these major dating sites were designed specifically to fit that need. For Jewish singles there's JDate, and Christian Mingle for all

Christian faiths. If this aspect is an important part of your dating criteria, then these sites are certainly a great place to start.

Creating Your Dating Profile

Once you have chosen which dating site(s) you would like to be a part of, it's time to carefully craft your online dating profile. Most sites have you fill out their standard questionnaire to help build your personal information and suggest potential matches. However, controlling how you answer questions and the amount of personal information you offer up is essential in both your protection and authenticity. If you do not answer questions honestly and represent yourself in an authentic way, the matches found for you simply won't pan out, because they are based only on a version of yourself.

Follow these tips to help create your best online dating profile:

- **Profile picture**. Choosing a flattering profile picture is crucial in finding the best possible matches. Regardless of where your self-esteem may be at in this point in time, it is vital that you choose a photo of yourself that is an accurate representation of how you look right now. Do not use a photo that is over 3 months old, and preferably one with no one else in the photo. Selfies can be acceptable as long as you actually look like yourself. One of the biggest complaints among online daters is that their potential match looks completely different in person than they did in their profile picture.

- **A cute screen name**. Choose a name for your online dating handle that is a good reflection of your personality and humor. A name that stands out is also a great way to attract potential matches to your profile. Try to go with something that incorporates your first and/or last name with one of your favorite things or a detail about you. For example, Jennifer Wilson from New York would seem fun and flirty with a screen name like "JennyintheCity82." It shows her nickname, that she is a city girl, and in this case, her birth year, 1982.

- **Basic information**. Never, ever, under any circumstances, lie about any aspect of your life. Do not claim to have a different job, higher education, or more luxurious lifestyle. Any dishonesty will inevitably come out when you find a match. The whole point of online dating is to put yourself out there and let the system do the work for you. Just like you would never lie about your job to someone's face on a date (or shouldn't!), the same set of rules apply to entering information on your e-dating profile.

- **What you're looking for**. Being honest about what you are hoping to find in a match is just as important as offering an authentic representation of yourself on your dating profile. When answering questionnaires on these sites, be both forthcoming and realistic with what you hope to find. Do not lower your standards, or set them too high. It is also helpful to give yourself a bit of wiggle room. If you think you are looking for a guy between the ages of 30 and 35, you may want to allow for potential matches beyond that age range. After all, does it really matter whether he is 35 or 38 if he is your perfect match?

The most important factors to remember when creating your online dating profile are to stay positive, be authentic, be kind, and be honest. Any negative aspects about you personally or comments on anything else are an instant turn-off to potential matches. Focus on the positive aspects of your life, personality, and interests; and you are sure to attract like-minded single guys.

How to Interact

So you have chosen a dating site, set-up your profile, and been alerted to potential matches. Now what? Interacting with other singles on dating sites is tricky, and must always be done with tact to avoid sending the wrong message or making hasty decisions before you know enough about someone. While it is extremely important to always be kind, there is a fine line between sparing someone's feelings when you are not interested and leading them on. Make sure you find that balance of being clear and polite.

There are many situations that arise when you put yourself out there on a dating site. You will get suggested matches that you have the option to contact, guys that see your profile and reach out to you, and guys you see that you would like to get in touch with. Enter each one of these situations with trepidation to avoid gaining a bad reputation or misleading someone that you are not interested in.

- **You get a notification that you have a possible match.** At this point, the ball is really in your court. Look carefully through each profile and compare the guy's attributes with your list of criteria. If the guy has an appealing profile picture, shares your interests, and fits your criteria, then it is up to you whether or not you want to reach out. This is where shyness and inhibitions can get in the way, so try approach the situation as you would if you were meeting someone in person. Send a short and sweet message explaining that you were matched up and that you are interested in learning more about him. There is no need to go into more detail. Just wait and see what kind of response you get.

- **While cruising your dating site, you find someone who peaks your interest.** When doing some digging yourself on dating sites, it is much easier to get caught-up in secondary details of someone's dating profile. Just because a guy has a great picture, good job, and lives in the area, doesn't automatically make him worth your time. If the site you use has not suggested this member as potential match for you, carefully read every detail of his profile to make sure it is worth your while to get in touch with him. Although he may look good on paper, having similar interests is vital in finding yourself a match, even if you're not looking for marriage. If he passes your initial screening, then send him the same type of message you would a guy that the site matches you up with.

- **You receive a message from a guy who is interested in you.** Whether you have already noticed him as a potential match or not, it is still crucial to investigate his entire profile before you respond to his message. The benefit of someone reaching out to you first, is that you should be able to get a bit of insight into his personality by how he words his introductory message. His profile information along with the tone of his message to you should be enough for you to tell how you would like to respond. If you are interested in him, respond with something casual and positive, agreeing that you two do seem to have a lot in common, and that you would love to talk more. Don't even rush into meeting someone face-to-face based on the initial message. On the other hand, if you are just not interested, kindly let him down in your response. Thank him for reaching out to you, and simply say you are focusing on other matches you think would work out better for you right now.

Protecting Yourself

Protecting yourself is vital when it comes to online dating. No matter how serious you are about finding Mr. Right, there is still information that should be kept off the record until you have spent enough time dating this guy in person. Once you do decide to meet-up with the cutie you have been messaging with back and forth, it is even more important to make sure you do not put yourself in a potentially dangerous situation.

- **Protect your identity**. Never, under any circumstances give out specific personal information. Saying the neighborhood you live in is fine, your exact address is not. Talking about your field and job title is great, but never reveal your salary. Basically if the information has numbers in it, be it your wages, address, social security number, or any other specific personal information, do not give it out. Online dating scammers can be both tricky and persuasive. No matter the reason, just keep identifying information to yourself.

- **Protect your friends and family**. Just as you wouldn't want to serve up your personal information on a silver platter, employ the same discretion with your family. There is no need to go down the list of every relative you have. How many siblings, cousins, or nieces you have is absolutely fine, but keep the names of your extended family and their locations under wraps until you actually want this guy to meet them!

- **Be smart and safe**. Once you decide you want to meet a potential match in person, certain precautions must be taken to ensure your physical safety. No matter how long you have been talking to this guy, you cannot be sure of anything about him, even if you have talked on the phone. You never truly know if his intentions are sincere or even if he is who he says he is, until you two get some substantial face time. When meeting-up with someone you met on a dating site, do not let him pick you up. Suggest meeting at the location of your date, and do not go home with him immediately after. If you are really dying to take him home with you, just make sure you are prepared either for him to turn on you and put you in a dangerous situation, or sleep with you and never call you again. The only way to ensure your safety is to stay in a public place for the entirety of your date.

- **Don't get Catfished!** For those unfamiliar with this term, being "Catfished" refers to people who go online to present themselves as someone completely different all together. This practice is becoming more and more commonplace, especially on Internet dating sites. It is a popular way for scammers to get people they meet online to send them money, or help them out in some way. Others, however, Catfish people simply for the thrill of pretending to be someone they wish they could be. If at any time something seems off or doesn't match up with what a guy has been telling you, try to find him on another site. Check social media sites like Facebook to see if there is someone with the same name and profile picture, with matching information. Learn more about how to spot a Catfish by watching *Catfish the Movie* or MTV's series, *Catfish*.

The best thing you can always remember to protect yourself both online and in person, is to trust your instincts. If you feel uneasy at any time, just remove yourself from the conversation or situation. When you finally do meet up with someone and they are not who they have claimed to be, you have every right to simply turn around and walk out the door with no further explanation.

Online Dating Pros and Cons

Just like conventional dating, there are both advantages and drawbacks to dating online. Use this list of Pros and Cons to online dating to help figure out if getting involved in online dating it's the right avenue for you:

Pros:

- **Saving Time.** Taking the time to fill out the initial questionnaires and set-up your online dating profile will undoubtedly save you time in the long-run. Being able to screen possible suitors online as opposed to weekly taking the time to get ready and spend hours on a date is a major advantage to young professionals.

- **Avoiding Awkwardness**. The ability to essentially "meet" and talk with someone before even going on a first date is helpful in avoiding those painful silences. You have already learned much more about each other's background, interests, and basic information than you would had you accepted a date from someone you met in a bar once before.

- **Convenience**. Being able to access your dating profile and matches 24/7 is helpful for those with odd schedules or work hours. Another convenient aspect of online dating is being able to meet other singles that share your interests, but may live just far enough away that wouldn't have the opportunity to ever run into each other in person.

Cons:

- **The Inaccurate Match**. Though each dating site has carefully calculated methods of matching singles, nothing is fool-proof. This is a part of why it is essential to screen each profile before talking to someone, in case the comput-

er, or you, have missed something undesirable.

- **The Dishonest Dater.** Whether you en-
counter a full-on Catfish or just a guy
who neglected to mention he is married, dating online means you run the
risk of getting involved with someone
you "think" you know, but really don't.
Even conventional dating requires time
and multiple dates to make sure the
person you are interested in is legiti-
mate, so only having e-mails, text mes-
sages, and phone calls to go off of can
leave a lot of details in question.

- **The Online Dating Rut.** Using an
online service to help find and screen
potential suitors can be extremely helpful at first, just be careful not to become
satisfied with solely online communication. For those shy or socially awkward
individuals, online dating can become a
way to get social interaction, and possible even a romantic relationship without ever having to spend time with
someone in person. Keep in mind, the
ultimate goal of online dating is to find
someone you physically want to be

with, not just talk to via electronic communication.

If you are considering entering the online dating scene, take the necessary time to ensure this is the best option for you. Online dating is never a substitute for conventional dating, just a different path you take to get there. Make sure you pick the right dating site, represent yourself in a positive, accurate way, and proceed with caution when it comes to talking to guys, and especially, meeting them in person.

Chapter 5 – Assessing a Potential Date

Not every date is a good date, and you will need to assess the good from the bad. Of course, the easiest thing to figure out is whether or not he floats your boat. Does he look good? Does he smell nice? How does he present himself in relation to your standards? Giving him the once-over is the first step to figuring out whether or not he's really worth dating. Never judge a book by its cover, but having someone that appears to take care of himself is an important factor.

A man who doesn't treat you well is never a good date. Pay close attention to whether or not he offers to pick up the check, whether he is in tune to the things that you say, and how he behaves towards you compared to other girls. Did you catch him eyeing other women? Well, if he does that on the first date, don't say yes to a second!

It takes men approximately 3 months to show their true colors. As important as it is to give a guy a chance, if the first date goes horribly wrong, that's typically a sign that nothing good is on the horizon. Some things are beyond anyone's control, such as the restaurant losing your reservation, bad service, or getting a flat tire. If any of these unlucky scenarios present themselves on your first date, at least it's a great way to get a sense of your guy's character by the way he handles it. However, if the date is bad due to specific actions on his part such as ogling other women, bad manners, or anything that makes you feel uncomfortable, don't bother giving him a second chance.

These types of behaviors are considered "Red Flags", or warning signs to abort the relationship immediately. Learning to spot these signs and handle the situation with care will be covered in more detail in Chapter 7.

Is He Really What You Want?

Sometimes, a match made in heaven is more or less a match made in hell. You might think you want something, but you don't really know until you have it. Dating a man for 3 months to 6 months can tell you volumes about whether or not you would actually be happy with having him as your boyfriend for the long term.

A good example of this is when Ms. Brainy decides to date Mr. Popular. More often than not, the geeky girl's introverted ways will cause a certain amount of friction with Mr. Popular's constantly packed social schedule. Though they may in fact love each other, but Mr. Popular isn't really what Ms. Brainy really would want in the grand scheme of things. It's easy to stay wrapped-up in adolescent fantasies of that hunky starting quarterback or Prom King even as an adult if you never got that experience. However, there comes a certain point where reality has to outweigh fantasy to find who you are actually compatible with.

One of the most difficult aspects of dating is being able to distinguish whether the guy you are dating is really what you want, or if you are just keeping him around for some other reason like an idealized fantasy, social status, or money.

Most of the time, you can tell whether or not this is the case because of a nagging feeling in the pit of your stomach, or a constant questioning in the back of your mind. Sometimes, it just manifests itself by the way that you behave with the date, or by the way that you react to the phone calls. A guy you truly see yourself with should make you excited to hear from him every single time he calls or texts. You should feel giddy or have butterflies in your stomach when you see him. These feelings are telltale signs of attraction, just be sure it isn't simply physical attraction. Though physical attraction is vital for long term relationships, expect everything to eventually fall apart if this is the only foundation you two have.

Signs that someone you are dating isn't really right for you tend to present themselves early. If you don't have any reaction to receiving a call or text or seeing your date, chances are you are missing that vital spark. A guy may be great on paper, but when you are with him, you know deep down you don't feel the way you really hoped to. The fact is that this is a very serious issue that you need to address. It's a matter of honesty. If you cannot be honest with yourself, you are not going to be able to be honest with your partner.

Worse still, if you end up committing to a person that you don't really want, you are going to make yourself (and likely your partner) miserable in the long term. If you aren't sure, give it a little more time. Test out different date scenarios to see what other common ground you may share and to get a better sense of his personality and character. If you know you are lying to yourself, then get out of that dating scene and get to the root of what is really causing you to do this. Not being honest with yourself is often a sign of underlying issues that need to be addressed.

Chapter 6 – What to Do If You Are Socially Awkward

If you are a socially awkward girl who gets anxious talking to new people and feels nervous in large social settings, then you probably find the realm of dating to be quite intimidating, and it's easy to see why. No other social interaction forces a woman to be more vulnerable emotionally (and physically) as dating. Don't miss out on meeting someone great simply because you are afraid of being in a potentially awkward or embarrassing situation. Remember, everyone feels that way at one time or another, even the most confident and outgoing individuals. It's impossible to always say the right thing at the right moment, but knowing how to roll with the punches and laugh at yourself can ease tension and even make you more attractive to your date.

Here are some tips that can help you cope with all the awkwardness that can come with being a shy girl in a not-so-shy world.

- When a girl apologizes for being shy or awkward, guys actually find it endearing. If you feel you may have said the wrong thing, or become internally flustered and can't find a response, try something like "Sorry! I always feel so awkward on first dates!" or "I'm a bit of an introvert, so sometimes it takes me a second to gather all of my thoughts!" Being honest diffuses awkward situations and shows your cute personality quirks. Don't be too afraid to use this tactic to break the ice with that hottie.

- When gearing-up for a first date, always have some kind of personal anecdote in your back pocket. A funny story from your childhood, an embarrassing story from college, or how you totally thought you blew an interview, but ended up getting the job. Learn a couple of jokes by heart, and start practicing them in front of the mirror. Anecdotes can be a good way to ease tension, increase your charm, and also show your friendly character. Being able to laugh at yourself makes you seem down to Earth, easy going, and most of all, real. Men love a girl who can make them laugh, and vice versa. Plus it encourages him to open up and share personal stories so you can get to know him better, as well.

- Calm down. A lot of the anxiety and anticipation you may experience before a date reduces the amount of fun that you actually have during the date. Don't miss out on the great parts of a first date because you are so wrapped up with anxiety in your own head. Plus, seeming nervous is an immediate turn-off. Remind yourself that he probably feels the same way, and first dates are hard for just about everyone. Be as present and involved as you can in the conversation, which will distract you from nagging voices in your head. If you really find yourself panicking, excuse yourself to the bathroom for a couple of deep breaths.

- One of the cruelest, meanest, and downright awful things that men often do to women who are obviously socially awkward or insecure is to pressure them into sex by trying to undermine what little self-esteem they may have. Should this happen at any point during a date, muster up your courage and walk out without saying a word. No one should ever make you feel uncomfortable or pressured for any reason. If you are questioning yourself about whether or not you are overreacting, you need to leave. Don't look back; that relationship was not going to go anywhere good.

- Being a Debbie Downer is not going to earn you plus points on any date. Don't schedule a date if you are not going to be in a cheerful and upbeat mood. If it's already set in stone, you could always cancel due to a scheduling conflict or the classic "something came up" excuse, and offer to reschedule with an added perk. Try "So sorry to cancel on you at the last minute, but is there any way we could reschedule for Saturday?

Drinks are on me!" This way the guy gets the message that it has nothing to do with him, and you avoid giving the wrong impression on the date. If you are down in the dumps but can't get out of the date, sometimes it helps to get a bit off your chest right off the bat. Say something like "It's so great to see you! I've had a horrendous day and have so been looking forward to having a nice dinner and relaxing!" This helps you move on without going into the nitty gritty details that can be a downer and shows you can take things in stride. Still need help perking up during a hot date? Smiling has been proven to improve a person's mood, whether or not it's a real smile.

- A major dating faux-pas is dressing inappropriately for the occasion. You don't want to send the wrong message by being overdressed, under dressed, or too scantily clad. Being too dressed-up could give the impression that you'd be a high maintenance girlfriend. Showing up under dressed could make it seem like you don't take pride in how you present yourself, or simply don't care about the date. If you are showing too much skin, via a low-cut neckline and tight mini-skirt, not only do you look like you are up for a one night stand, but you are inviting other guys to ogle you when you are already out with someone. Heels and a nice dress are always appropriate for an evening date, just choose one area of your body to play-up with exposed skin or tight clothing. Daytime dates should be a bit more casual. If you love heels, try a wedge or lower height with denim and cute top.

- Keep makeup to a minimum. Believe it or not, men do not like the "clown face" look that many women glob on. Ideally, makeup will hide flaws and accentuate your best features. Make sure your foundation and/or powder are the right for your skin tone, so you look as natural as possible. Keep colors flattering to your skin, and not too bright or heavy-handed. If you are not usually the make-up wearing type, even out skin tone with a bit of foundation, add a soft blush and a swipe of mascara. Play-up your look a bit for evening dates with a slightly darker lipstick or eye shadow, but not both. Just like your outfit, your make-up should focus on playing-up your best feature.

- Don't ever lie on a first date. It will not end well. Either your date will fall in love with a fake you, or you will get caught in a lie later on in the relationship. Either way, it doesn't put you off to a great start. If you just blurt something out, try to backtrack right away, and be prepared to laugh at yourself so it just seems like a slip, and not an intentional deception. Never feel as though you need to fabricate any details about yourself or your life to hook a guy. The relationship will never work out if you are not being completely authentic.

- Confidence is the number one turn on when it comes to men. Be confident, and stand proudly! Try not to go overboard, which can make you seem arrogant, but humbly offer up accomplishments when it fits into the conversation, and always try to stay positive, even when discussing a sensitive subject. If you aren't confident, don't worry! Take after the old adage, and "fake it till you make it."

- The easiest way to scare off a guy is to bring up "marriage" or "children" as key words during a first date. At this point, it's too soon to tell if these kinds of discussions will send a guy running in the opposite direction. There is no harm in going out with a guy several times only to find out he never wants to have kids, and you do. Certainly don't waste a year dating someone without knowing you want the same things in life, but when you are just getting to know someone, there shouldn't be a rush. Even if you feel anxious to move on to marriage and a family in your own life, the right guy will fit into your plans whether you talk about it on the first or tenth date. Most men want to take those subjects slowly, and bringing them up in the first couple of dates will reek of desperation. Don't sabotage after yourself; keep that claptrap shut!

- Don't only talk about yourself. Learn about your prospective partner during those first couple of dates. It will be useful when you decide whether or not he is worth your time. Plus, you would find your date tedious, boring, and even arrogant if all he did was talk about himself the entire time. Naturally, that feeling goes both ways.

- Are you a career woman who simply can't get into the dating mindset? Then, treat your first date like a job interview. Have a couple of questions that you want to know, a couple of answers to typical questions, and let it go from there. Write your questions down with a pen and paper to help them stick in your mind, and re-read them before you head out for your date. Even better, do some research on your date by taking a look through his social media profiles to see what he is interested in. This is a great way to have conversation starters ready.

- Remember, dating is all about fun. Sure, there are going to be awkward moments, pauses in the conversation, and a bit of nervousness, but they are all part of the experience. Try to relax and appreciate that both of you are putting yourselves out there. He wouldn't have asked you out if he didn't like you or find you attractive, so keep that mind. Putting too much pressure on either yourself or your date can instantly kill the fun vibe. If you are not having fun, you are not doing it right!

- Don't be afraid to ask other friends for useful dating advice if you are the "awkward girl" in your group. After all, the more information that you have in your arsenal, the better off you will be when you finally hit the dating scene. Go out to a bar with a handful of girlfriends and see how they react when approached by a guy. Study their body language, key phrases, and what criteria they use to decide if they want to give him their number or not. While you may not agree with how they operate, it is still a great learning experience to help you evaluate your own dating prowess.

Chapter 7 – Red Flags to Watch Out For

If you are reading this book, you might have already experienced some of these signs showing that the guy you're dating has some major issues. Knowing how to recognize them and when to make a run for it is crucial in helping to avoid a terrible relationship, or perhaps even an abusive one. Many women continue to stay in relationships despite warning signs of dysfunction or abuse for a variety of reasons. Maybe they are scared of being alone, afraid of how the guy will retaliate after the break-up, or have such low self-esteem that they actually believe it's alright to be treated poorly. Whatever the case, no one should ever be treated with less than total dignity, respect, and consideration. If you see signs early on that this could be the case, don't wait around to find out.

Here are some red flags that should signal "end of relationship," if not "end of date."

- He belittles you, makes negative comments about your clothing, looks, or family. This is a major sign of disrespect, and it will not stop after the first date. The first time it happens, make a point of letting him know how it made you feel. If he apologizes profusely and it doesn't happen again, fine. If it does happen again, cut the cord immediately. There is no excuse.

- He asks you to come over, you to pay for his dinner, you to basically do everything for the date. Whether this guy is looking for a mother figure or just plain lazy, chances are he is not going to be pulling his own weight in the relationship – romantically, financially, or otherwise.

- You get the nagging feeling that he is using you for sex. If this thought even enters your mind, it's probably true. Try telling him you'd like to slow things down a bit, or just don't spend the night with him and see how he takes it. If he stops calling, there's your answer.

- He seems terrified of being seen holding hands with you in public, or anything similar to that. Some people just are not into PDA, which is totally fine. Although, it can't really hurt to ask. You don't want to overlook a warning sign that this guy could be embarrassed to be seen with you, has intimacy issues, or worst of all, is married. There is a difference between not wanting to be inappropriate in public and purposely trying to look inconspicuous.

- You don't know what it is, but something just seems to be "off" about this guy. You don't need to be able to pinpoint the reason or cause. Trust your gut. There have been women who married serial killers because they didn't.

- Did you just catch him in a lie? On the first date? Run. If he isn't honest with you from the start, what makes you think he will be honest with you by day three? Or day 503?

- Somehow, it seems like every single last date he has been on has been with a horrible woman. You know better. It's unlikely that all of his past three girlfriends were psycho, cheaters, or the like. Besides, if this really is the case, you don't want to be associated with this group of exes. Either way, it's bad news. Remember, if he is going around calling his exes those names, he will call you the same ones when he's done dating you.

- Has he admitted to hitting his exes? Are there cases against him which involve abuse? Does he even joke about a woman needing to be "put in her place"? There is no justification for any kind of abuse, and it's never appropriate or funny to joke about it. Don't give this guy another thought. Just leave.

- Any man with stalking charges, assault charges, or similar felony charges is NOT a catch. There is no sob story that could possibly excuse this kind of behavior. In fact, you should probably run very far from anyone like this.

- Watch how your potential man behaves with the waiter. A good guy will treat your waiter with dignity. A red flag would be hurling abuse at the poor waiter, or crassly asking for a discount. Remember, if he will do that to an innocent waiter, he will do that to you, too. The way someone treats a stranger can speak volumes about their character.

- Never go on a second date with a man who compares you to other women. This is just purely disrespectful, unnecessarily mean behavior. Whether it's his own insecurities or trying to find yours, it's definitely not something you even want to talk about on a first date, or you know, ever.

- If he seems to be putting in no effort to making a first date wonderful or exciting, don't expect him to put much effort into anything in the future. There is nothing wrong with a traditional dinner and a movie date. However, if he takes you to a casual spot where he goes after work every day anyway, he is obviously not trying to make much of an effort.

- Do you get the feeling that he is trying to change you already? Don't stick around to find out. This is a sign of controlling behavior that needs to be dealt with before it's too late.

- If he never moved out of his parents' house, and he's over the age of 30, it's a red flag. Enough said.

- Is he constantly late or simply just not showing up for dates? Then forget about him. This is often a sign that you are the other woman, or just not his priority. If he doesn't take your time seriously, don't take his seriously.

- Does your date seem to have a horror story divorce...or three? Too many divorces can be a serious sign of deep-seeded issues. The more baggage he has in terms of ex-wives or baby's mamas, the more these women are always going to be a part of your life, and possibly try to undermine your relationship.

- Sometimes, a really big sign of mental instability is the sign of being an animal lover. We aren't talking normal animal attachments – we are talking about the dates who won't even leave the house without their pet, and talk about them constantly as if they are a child. Caring for animals and wanting to be a parent is definitely desirable. However, un-necessary attachments can be due to underlying issues that are almost never good.

- Your date will need a job. Let's face it, even in this tough economy, it will not do you any good to have a boyfriend or husband who doesn't pull his weight around the house. Meeting someone who is just out of college or in-between jobs is one thing, but if your date has been out of work for more than two months, it's likely he will stay unem-ployed for a few more.

- Single fathers are awesome...unless their children seem to be spoiled rotten. You don't want to inherit these issues when you start dating, so why date men who raise their children poorly?

This is the best way to tell if he would be a good parenting partner for you in the future, and if you already disagree with how he is raising his kids, it won't be any different when it's your child, too. Plus, if his kids won't like you, the relationship is doomed to fail.

- Does your date's mom still call the shots in his love life? This isn't only a sign of serious mental issues; it's a sign that you should back away. Dating a mama's boy is not advisable under most circumstances, and you don't want to waste time if the mother is one of those who believe no woman is "good enough" for her son.

Getting Out

Dating red flags are a sign that something is very, very wrong. Most of the time, running into red flags on a date can be a precursor to abusive, neglectful, unfaithful, or just plainly unstable behavior from your suitor down the line. Avoiding relationships with red flags is not only a way to ensure that you won't be hurt in the future by a bad boyfriend, but it is also a matter of safety that you need to be aware of. Whether it is your mental, emotional, or physical well-being at stake, you should never feel compromised for the sake of any relationship.

It should be noted that guys with abusive tendencies also exhibit a lot of manipulative behavior, and once you are in a serious relationship, it can be a lot more subtle, so be very aware in of things that seem odd in the beginning. Some of these guys exhibit red flags on purpose in order to "test" their dates. It could be something as simple as underhandedly insulting your family, or innocently asking you to pay on the first date because he "forgot his wallet." If the guy is being genuine, you should be able to tell.

Many times, women who were in abusive relationships, once they have gotten out of the vicious cycle, talk about how they "should have noticed the warning signs" at the start of their old relationships. Does this sound like a musing that you want to have in the future? Probably not. Guard yourself against these scumbags, and don't say yes to a 2nd date with a red flagger.

Take precautions on the first date such as not revealing your home address, meeting at the location of your date instead of being picked-up, and staying in public places. This way you protect yourself and can make a clean break from the red flagger. Even if he seems angry or threatening, the most he can do is keep calling you, at which point you can just block him, and/or change your number. If you end up alone with him, chances are he is bigger and stronger than you are, putting you at a disadvantage to defend yourself. Just don't end up alone with a guy until you have had a few dates with him, and ideally met a few of his friends, coworkers, or family members.

Chapter 8 – So, The First Date's Over. Now What?

After you have your first date, it's time to sit down and go over what went right and what went wrong. This will help reveal your true feelings and ultimately decide if it's worth your time to see this person again.

Ask yourself how the date made you feel, whether you have noticed any red flags that might have upset you, as well as whether or not you felt that special spark with your potential date. After all, if you didn't enjoy the first date, there is going to be a pretty big chance that you won't enjoy the second or the third. The choice, for the most part, is up to you.

How much did you smile and laugh? What traits does he have that you would like to see in your ideal mate? Did he exhibit any red flags? Does he have any qualities or lifestyle choices that you do not like? Are you attracted to him? If all of these answers are positive, then you should be excited to see him again! If he seems great and you are attracted to him, but something is holding you back, consider if previous relationship hang-ups are affecting your current dating choices, and deal with them now before you miss out on someone who could potentially be right for you.

One of the things that many women need to remember is that you don't owe men anything. If the guy is pressuring you into date #2, and it just doesn't seem like you are into him, don't go. Going out with a guy out of pity, fear, or just plain boredom is not a good enough reason, and wastes both his time and yours. Besides which, he will be more hurt if you break it off after five dates rather than one. Is he not taking rejection too well? Just rant about it to a friend. It helps reduce stress, and also can be fun.

Another thing that you need to do is to congratulate yourself. Go ahead. Give yourself a pat on the back. Dating isn't an easy thing for anyone, even those who seem to be social butterflies. Whether you think you have met your future husband or pray you never see this guy again, be proud of yourself for going, putting yourself out there, and being open.

Relax, give yourself a treat, or just laugh it off. It's important to offer yourself positive reinforcement for pursuing the things you want in life.

Although you have the majority of the power, you have to gauge the attraction that the guy feels for you, too. Is he calling, texting, or just dropping a line on Facebook? If so, then he probably wants a second or a third date. If he isn't showing a sign of life, or worse, telling you he isn't interested, don't press the issue. It is in your best interest to continue along your search for Mr. Right, and not take it too personally. Just because a guy doesn't want to take you out again doesn't mean you did anything wrong, or that there is anything wrong with you. Don't waste your time and energy going over the date in your mind to figure out why he is not interested. The reason is irrelevant, the point is that he is clearly not right for you, so the best thing you can do is accept it, and move on.

Not sure whether or not he is interested? Well, you have two options when it comes to figuring this stuff out. The first option is to wait, and for women who are a little bit more old-fashioned, this is usually a good way to figure out whether or not he is interested. As a general rule, if he doesn't call within 3 days, he probably isn't interested in dating you again.

If you are more upfront, (and many men actually appreciate this) then asking him flat-out is a good way to get a straight answer. This actually could also boost your chances of seeing him again if done correctly. Just give a subtle text thanking him for the great night, and asking him if he wants to meet up again. If you reach out to him a day or two after the date and don't hear back, just let it go.

Does He Actually Want To Meet Up Again?

If he does the following, he doesn't want to meet up with you again. Or, he is just not into you for a serious thing.

- *He is calling you at odd hours of the night.* This almost always signals a booty-call, which is not what you want if you are trying to really date and get to know this guy.

- *You are getting the feeling he isn't taking you seriously.* Whether he is not respecting your time, effort, or really paying attention to you, it doesn't feel great, even if you are only interested in dating him casually. So don't waste your time.

- *He seems to be avoiding your calls, or cutting them short.* Unless you are calling him when he is at work, there is no real reason for this rude behavior. If you get any inclination that he is not into talking to you, he is not into dating you, either.

- *There just never seems to be enough time to meet you at the diner, or at the park.* If he keeps offering reasons as to why he can't meet up with you, chances are they are just excuses. When you are really into someone, you make the time, so don't waste yours waiting around for him.

- *You find out he is dating other women.* Even if you are only looking for something more casual, knowingly dating someone who is seeing other people increases your risk for STDs, drama, and potentially heartbreak. You may think you are OK with it at first, but if you do end up feeling strongly about this guy, you already can't completely trust him, and that is no way to start a relationship.

Do You Actually Want To Meet Up With Him Again?

If you exhibit the following signs during a date, then you don't really want to see him again.

- *You are making up excuses for his behavior, no matter how bad it gets during a date.* If you have to try too hard to figure someone out, it's most likely not worth your time and effort. Finding someone's behavior odd is not really the way you want to feel on a date.

- *You were grossed out by his eating manners.* Bad manners are inexcusable. Period.

- *The date just left you flat...no feeling, no loss, nothing.* If you don't feel that spark with someone right off the bat, you can pretty much bet it's not going to magically appear after the second- or tenth date.

- *You felt embarrassed about being seen with him during the date.* No matter the reason, if you were embarrassed to be seen with someone, why would you go out with them again?

- *Something just seemed off.* This gut feeling could be the signal of a red flagger, or just that you really don't see the relationship going anywhere. Always trust this feeling. Your intuition knows best-even after just one date.

Getting To the Second Date

The second date is often a lot easier to reach than the first. In fact, it's as easy as asking for it. It's also worth mentioning that second dates are more casual than first dates, but should still be taken seriously. It takes up to 3 months to fully see a person's character, so you should be on alert for anything that seems off color to you. Someone can easily be on their best behavior on a first date, and start to slip into bad habits on the second. Sometimes these personality quirks don't show themselves for weeks, or even months, but that's why waiting to get really involved with someone is always the smarter way to go.

Usually both parties are at least a bit nervous on the first date, so use the second date as an opportunity to get a bit more in depth and learn as much as you can about your suitor. Each date should reveal a bit more about his background, lifestyle, personality, and what he is looking for in life in general. If you don't feel you are getting to know him much better, chances are he is holding back for some reason, and you could be wasting your time. If he is not willing to open up to you, he is probably not looking for a relationship.

If all goes well on the second date, you may be in luck! Keep your eyes open for warning signals and red flags, especially until you become monogamous, but typically if the first two or three dates go very well, you might be looking at a serious relationship, or potential husband.

Chapter 9 – The Thrill of the Chase...Keeping Your Man

Having a first or second date is great, but the fact is that healthy relationships take years to cultivate, and one too many issues can break even the strongest of bonds. In order to actually keep the guy that you are dating, you are going to have to put in a lot of effort. Dating is never easy, and getting him to be a long term boyfriend is even more difficult. Are you ready to take on that challenge?

Once you have been consistently dating for about 3 months, it's time to evaluate the relationship. By this time you should have a good idea of how you really feel about this guy, and where you would personally like the relationship to go. It is important, however, to be blatantly honest and make sure you are both on the same page to avoid either person's feelings being hurt. Make sure you are being honest with yourself, and collect your thoughts before you have the Big Talk where you establish what you would both like out of the relationship.

Here are some questions you should ask yourself to clarify what you really want, before you see where he is at:

- How strong are your feelings at this point? After a couple of months, it should be easy enough to tell if you are really falling head over heels for this guy. If you don't think your feelings are growing stronger, this is probably not a long-term relationship for you.

- What are you looking for moving forward? If you are having a great time together, and developing strong feelings for this guy, it's time to ask yourself the tough questions. Could you see yourself marrying him? Do you think he would be a good father? If you are looking for a husband and someone to raise children with, you need to be honest with yourself about what you want so you can make that clear to him.

- What do you value most in life? Is family and friends? Is it cultivating a successful career and financially stable lifestyle? Knowing what you want to focus on in life and the type of lifestyle you hope to lead will help you figure out if you and your significant other's goals match up.

Getting on the Same Page

The first thing that you have to do is have the Big Talk. This is the talk where you establish where your boundaries for cheating are, what you want in a relationship, and whether or not you are actually an official couple.

Going into this conversation having already established what you are looking for in your own mind is crucial. You need to stand firmly on what you want, and not be swayed by your guy's opinions. If you compromise something you know you want just to keep the relationship going, it will end with you being unhappy.

Being upfront about these matters will make sure that you don't confuse anything later on in your relationship. Many couples have broken up because of these misunderstandings, and you don't want to put your relationship in jeopardy by assuming things.

Honestly is the foundation for any strong relationship, and if your views differ in what you want out of life, it's better to address it now rather than a year or two down the road. Some marriages even end in divorce simply because one person thought the other would change their mind about lifestyle choices, such as wanting to have children.

Most people who have successful relationships say that having common goals helps bring couples closer together. Do you and your boyfriend have a common goal, such as having a family, a home, or a company? Common goals come in all sorts of different shapes and sizes, so make sure to find some.

The Deal Breakers

Deal breakers are major issues that cannot be agreed upon by both parties. These issues need to be discussed before the relationship gets serious, to avoid a painful break-up or worse, divorce down the line. Since you have already asked yourself these questions before going into the conversation with your man, it is simply a matter if seeing that the things you want in life match up.

- Do you want to get married?

- Do you want to have children?

- Where do you see yourself living for the next 10 years? Where would you want to retire?

- How important is sharing the same religion and/or spirituality?

- What are your current and future financial goals?

- Which activities or hobbies would you like to pursue in the future?

Once you have both discussed these "big picture" issues, it should be very clear whether or not you two are compatible for the long term. Just make sure you are not compromising what you really want in life. If you have your heart set on getting married and starting a family, but he is looking for a life of freedom and travel, it is in your best interest to cut your losses and move on until you find someone who wants the same things you want.

Preventing Infidelity

Common interests are also very important when it comes to keeping your love life healthy. If you two drift apart, it's very possible that differing interests are to blame. Try to keep at least 5 or 6 major interests in your life that you have in common with your significant other, and make the effort to partake in them regularly. This way, you will have your daily (or weekly) bonding sessions with your love, and greatly lower your risk of drifting apart. It also forces you to prioritize each other and spend quality time together, which is a great habit to start early-on. Getting in the mindset that quality time together is a priority will enhance your relationship in the future. Marriage, kids, work, and keeping up with your family and his, only leaves less time for you two to connect, and those couples who have set a precedent of reserving time together are most successful.

You also need to take care of yourself and take time for yourself. Those "joined at the hip" couples that you often see snuggling don't really last too long, and that actually can be a sign of codependency issues that need to be resolved. Showing affection and spending as much time together as possible is wonderful, but it can also lead to becoming unnecessarily annoyed with each other. If you are always together and don't have the chance to miss each other, it becomes too easy to take each other for granted. Make sure you also reserve time for friends, family, and yourself.

Taking care of yourself will also ensure that you remain attractive. Sad to say, a lot of guys do stray when they notice that women no longer take care of themselves. Putting effort into maintaining your physical fitness, health, appearance, and hygiene not only increases your own self-esteem, but keeps your partner interested.

You need time for yourself, and you also need to pay attention to what you need in the relationship. Don't ever lose yourself in another person. Otherwise, the qualities you have that originally attracted your partner to you can disappear, and the same can happen for him. No one should get to the point where they are complacent about their relationship, or feel like the no longer know who they are as an individual. Lifelong bonds take work, effort, and cooperation to ultimately be successful.

Never stop making an effort for your partner. If you feel that something has changed, or he is showing less interest, ask what he is feeling and try to get to the root of the issue. It may be something personal that has nothing to do with you. However, sometimes even personal issues and internal conflict can lead someone down the path to infidelity when overlooked. If one of you is feeling lost, it is the other's job to be a supportive partner and help the other work through whatever problems they may be facing with compassion and an open mind.

If you make a visible effort to look and feel your best, spend quality time with one another, and address problems as soon as they arise, chances are your relationship will continue to be monogamous and successful. Always find ways to show love, support, and gratitude for your partner, and it will get you the same in return.

Men are visual creatures, and they love variety. Smart women often will try to put on another persona in bed once in a while in order to make sure that their guy stays attracted to them. Spicing things up, and keeping things new will make sure that guys will not take you for granted. One of the most common reasons for men to cheat is because they are bored with what they have at home. Do you really want to be in a monotonous relationship, anyway? Probably not.

Don't Be Taken For Granted!

You also have to make sure that you aren't a doormat, and this is very hard for some women to do. It is second nature to many women to say "yes" to their guys, and to forgive issues that they know they shouldn't forgive. When men are given too much leeway, they forget what a great thing it is to have you as a girlfriend. Don't let yourself be taken for granted by the man that you love; learn to say no. If necessary, kick them to the curb.

Another very vital lesson for women is to learn when enough is enough. We have all heard about that one friend who says she is going to leave her cheating husband "when the time is right," but that time never comes. We also know when a relationship is toxic, even if we don't really want to admit what is going on. Sometimes, as much as we want to keep the guys we are with, we shouldn't and can't. Mr. Right should be right for you, and if he is making life hell, the he isn't Mr. Right.

You know when you are not happy, so you are doing yourself a disservice by ignoring those feelings. Everyone deserves to be happy, and no one deserves to be treated poorly. If at any time you experience mental, emotional, verbal, or physical abuse from your partner, do not hesitate to end the relationship. Life is too short to stay with someone that makes you unhappy for ANY reason!

Chapter 10 – Marriage Material?

If you have been dating for a while, it's time to start asking yourself where the relationship is going. Those who are marriage-minded need to find out whether or not their boyfriend views the idea of marriage as a possibility. If neither of you is really into the idea of marriage or kids, that's totally fine, but if one person has been assuming the other shares their viewpoint and it's not true, you could have a rocky break-up ahead.

These days, getting married isn't a must – many couples forgo the idea completely. Divorce rates in the US, and even in countries like India where it is not as accepted, are skyrocketing. Getting married is a major, major step that should not be taken lightly. Though divorce is more common than ever, it should never be seen as a "way out" of the marriage if it doesn't work out. Divorce is still an extremely painful and often scarring process, especially if you have children involved. If you have any doubts that things may not work out down the road, do NOT go through with a wedding. When deciding whether or not he is marriage material you have to be as serious and objective as possible. After all, that means you will probably spend the rest of your life with him, which essentially puts your well-being in his hands.

Many women make the mistake of broaching the subject too frequently, or too quickly. Though it is important to have a conversation about what you would want in the future, dating for six months isn't usually a good time frame for demanding a ring. Most of the time, couples will date for several years before a proposal is made, regardless both of their ages.

However, if you are a woman who really wants to get married, it's alright to say so, just make sure you are saying it in a way that is expressing your feelings, rather than putting pressure on your man. Even if you are feeling antsy to tie the knot, telling your boyfriend you are going to end the relationship if you don't receive a proposal is pretty unreasonable. There really are no healthy marriages that start with an ultimatum. Instead, try to voice your opinions on marriage and children, and see how he reacts. You never know what kind of plans he has, and don't want to ruin the surprise of a marriage proposal because you keep pushing the issue.

Try your best to be patient, and if you have a strong feeling the relationship may not be going anywhere, set a time limit in your own mind. For those over 30 who want to start a family, give him another year or so to pop the question. If nothing progresses in that time frame, make it clear that you need to end the relationship to have the chance to find someone who wants the same things you do. If you are still in your 20s, and happily in love, then it's probably in your best interest to just wait it out.

If you are thinking about marrying the guy, you need to make sure that you are reading the signals correctly. Is he really the commitment type? Does he want to commit to *you*? Check for these signs that it's getting very serious.

- **You have moved in together**. If you move in together, chances are much higher that he is in it for the long haul, and wants you by his side. The first year of living together is a good trial period for marriage. Being in love doesn't necessarily mean you are suited to living together, which is part of ultimate compatibility.

- **It's been 5 years**. This is usually the benchmark that many guys use to propose. If not 2 years, that is. If he isn't the timeline kind of guy, it might be that he will propose after a major life event, such as graduating college or getting that big promotion. If either of you are unsure you want to spend the rest of your lives together after 5, or even 2 years, it's more likely than not that it's just not meant to be.

- **He's introduced you to his extended family, and his mom has taught you family recipes**. This means that the parents really are expecting you two to get hitched. At this point, you are family, and not just the girlfriend. Just don't get too ahead of yourself. His family may love you, and you them, but don't assume it is because he has clued them in to some master plan. The two of you still need to communicate to each other what you are looking for out of life.

- **He has started talking about rings, or asking you where you want the relationship to go**. He is testing the waters to make sure that you will say yes when he asks you if this is the case. Any talk of marriage from a guy is usually a sign that you are officially commitment-oriented in your relationship.

- **It's not only you he is serious about**. Men who are also serious about their careers often want a wife, too. Just don't confuse a career-minded man with a committed one. There can be a fine line between being dedicated to your work and a work-a-holic. You still want to choose a mate that will always make time for you, and for a family if that is what you both want.

If he is interested in marrying, don't jump in just yet. Before you say "I do," it's a good idea to look for the following signs to make sure that your matrimony isn't a mistake that could lead to a painful divorce.

- **You don't feel stifled by him, and you don't feel like you are scared of disappointing him**. You should never feel smothered or trapped by a husband. If you are feeling this way now, things are not going to improve in the future if you get married. In fact, they will most likely get worse. Aiming to please and being able to compromise are certainly desirable qualities, just make sure you don't go overboard. You should always feel free to be yourself, and have a partner that supports your dreams and interests. It is also crucial that you are not afraid to go out on a limb, and that your spouse will be there to catch you if you fall.

- **You are willing to withstand (and have already withstood) his most annoying quirks**. You will have to withstand them for the rest of your life. Learning to pick your battles now will only help you live together harmoniously in the future. Don't sweat the small stuff just as much as you don't let the big things go. Whether you pick fights over every little thing, or ignore warning signs of irresponsibility–or worse, infidelity, under or overreacting can quickly lead to unhappiness and the end of a relationship. Voice opinions when something major bothers you, but don't nag him about every little annoying habit.

- **Both of you are financially stable**. Money can't buy you love, but it can prevent divorce. Financial issues are the number one reason why divorces occur in the United States. Make sure you are both on the same page with financial goals, spending habits, and shared responsibilities. After all, if you are going to get married, having a wedding is one of the hugest expenses you will undertake in your entire life. If you don't already have a solid financial foundation in place, the wedding planning alone could be your undoing.

- **Both of you know what kind of life you want to live, and can actually agree on it**. If you are a beer and hotdogs girl, and he is a filet mignon and caviar kind of guy, there is going to be a culture clash. Agreeing on the type of lifestyle you would like to lead is something that must be done together. Before you get married, you should both have a clear picture of where you would like to live, if you plan on buying property or renting, and what activities and people will take priority. Picturing completely different lifestyles will definitely not end well.

Marriage, as a whole, is not something to be taken lightly. You need to make sure that there is a lot of thought put into that decision; otherwise you will probably have to pay a lot of high prices in order to undo that wedding vow.

No matter how badly you have dreamed of getting married, just because you are in a serious relationship doesn't mean you have to take the plunge. Being brutally honest with yourself is vital in determining if the guy you are with is truly the person you want to wake up next to every single day for the rest of your life. If there is even one nagging voice in the back of your mind, listen to it. Those who go through with a marriage in lieu of hesitations pretty much always end up getting divorced. If you think it's hard dating now, it won't be any easier when you are five years older and a single mom with two children.

Always be true to yourself, and respect what your partner wants. If he just isn't looking for the same lifestyle, cut your losses while you can. Walk away from the relationship with dignity and perspective to start anew and continue looking for the life you have always dreamed of. You deserve to be happy, so give yourself the opportunity to find what you know you truly want.

Conclusion

Navigating today's dating world is harder than ever. Getting out there may seem like the hardest part, but staying smart in the dating scene can be an equally daunting task. Before you are even ready to put yourself out there, it is important to have a good idea of what you are looking for, and have the self-assurance to feel good about yourself. If you have underlying issues either personally or due to past relationships, it will undoubtedly affect your current love life. Feeling confident in both yourself and what you hope to find in a partner will help streamline the dating process and keep you on track.

Make sure you are looking for guys in the places that are best suited to your interests and personality. Decide if online dating is right for you, or not, and seek advice from friends, especially those who have successful, committed relationships. Everyone's story is different, but learning from others is always valuable and offers insight into how you conduct your own love life. Take each person's advice and perspective with a grain of salt, and try to see where they are coming from. It can only help in better understanding your dates when you are in the situation.

On those first couple of dates it is important to present yourself well, and make a good first impression. Be yourself, for sure, just make sure you are not dominating the conversation, nor holding back. Try to relax, maintain your confidence and keep nagging voices in your head from getting the best of you. Remind yourself that we are all human, everyone gets nervous, and everyone makes mistakes. Learn to laugh at yourself when necessary, and look for the positive aspects of every person and situation.

There may be times when you find yourself in a situation you did not anticipate, and you need to get out. It takes months to really get to know someone, and often times, deal breakers don't appear until you have already invested a certain amount of time and care into a relationship. However, trusting your instincts is the best way to handle any situation. If you get even the slightest inclination that something is off, it might be time to walk away. Waiting it out to see if things will improve is almost always a waste of time for both parties involved.

Once you start dating someone and it is going well, don't jump the gun. It's all too easy to get caught-up in future visions of weddings, babies, and growing old together. However, getting into this frame of mind too soon could ultimately jeopardize the entire relationship. The guy you are dating very well could be the future father of your children, but if he feels like he is being pressured to commit before he is ready, you could lose him completely. Patience is a virtue in dating, so no matter how old you are or your future romantic aspirations, allow enough time for both of you to get on the same page.

If you think you have found The One, hold on to him. Carefully assess each step in your relationship, like when you are ready to become exclusive, move-in together, and hopefully, get engaged. Approach these subjects with tact, compassion, and understanding, and you will have the best chance of getting the same back from your partner. Relationships take compromise, especially to be successful for the long term.

Dating is unpredictable, just like people. Though the advice outlined in this book is helpful, there is no be-all, end-all formula for being successful in the dating world. The only things we can know for sure are that being true to yourself and honest with your potential partner are vital in finding someone who is right for you. Never compromise your standards and never stay with someone if you are unhappy in any way.

Use this guide as inspiration to put your best foot forward when it comes to dating, and pursue happiness in finding the love you have always wanted. Refer to the many tips, tricks, and potential missteps herein when you feel lost or unsure of what to do next. Hopefully it will serve you well, and lead you straight to Mr. Right!

CPSIA information can be obtained at www.ICGtesting.com
Printed in the USA
BVOW02s0240150515

400536BV00007B/28/P